STO

FRIENDS
OF ACPL

72
Showcase of interior design

Ed

DO NOT REMOVE
CARDS FROM POCKET

4-29-91

ALLEN COUNTY PUBLIC LIBRARY

FORT WAYNE, INDIANA 46802

You may return this book to any agency, branch,
or bookmobile of the Allen County Public Library.

DEMCO

SHOWCASE OF INTERIOR DESIGN ™

Forty-Three Designers
and Their Work
Midwest Edition

Vitae Publishing, Inc.
Grand Rapids, MI

Allen County Public Library
Ft. Wayne, Indiana

Copyright © 1989 Vitae Publishing, Inc.

All rights reserved under International
and Pan-American Copyright Conventions.
Published in the United States
by Vitae Publishing, Inc.
800 Grand Plaza Place
Grand Rapids, MI 49503

Chairman, John C. Aves
President, James C. Markle

Library of Congress
Cataloging-in-Publication Data

Pool, Mary Jane.
   Showcase of interior design.

   1. Interior decoration firms—Illinois—Chicago.
2. Interior decoration firms—Illinois. 3. Interior
decoration—Illinois—Chicago—History—20th century.
4. Interior decoration—Illinois—History—20th century.
I. Aves, John C., 1942-   . II. Harris, William R.,
1951-   . III. Title.
NK2004.P66 1989   729'.025'77311   89-51668
ISBN 0-9624596-0-7
ISBN 0-9624596-1-5 (soft)

PROJECT STAFF

For Vitae Publishing, Inc.
Concept, Design and Production,
Aves Advertising, Inc.

Contributing Editor, Mary Jane Pool
Publisher, Gita M. Gidwani
Marketing Assistant, Susan LeTourneau

Pre-production, printing and binding,
R.R. Donnelley & Sons Company

Chicago, Illinois

Title Page Interior Design: Bruce Gregga
Photo: Tony Soluri

TABLE
OF
CONTENTS

TABLE
OF
CONTENTS

TABLE
OF
CONTENTS

A personal journey through the world of interior design.

By Mary Jane Pool

*M*y appreciation of wizards of the interior began when I was a child. Mother always had Mr. Folsom to get things done, to make rooms pretty and comfortable. He knew where to find the right Kiva rug, the perfect Pembroke table, the deliciously faded blue and white blocked linen for curtains. My father once dreamed we painted the living room raspberry red with white moldings, and so we did. It was wonderful for years.

*W*hen I arrived at *Vogue* Magazine in the mid 1940's, right out of college, Joseph Platt had just redesigned the reception room in pale woods and slim, tailored upholstery typical of that period. There were still some signs of the earlier Elsie de Wolf decoration. The office of Edna Woolman Chase, the editor-in-chief, was a vision of delicate color, with small scale French furniture and a charming crystal chandelier. In the 1960's designer Billy Baldwin was called in to bring the reception room up to date. He covered the Platt sofas in a cotton printed in apple green and white, scattered around lots of basket chairs, enough for lunch parties and large seminars. As the room was circled with windows and opened onto terraces it was like a garden in the sky and a surprise and delight for all who came to see us. The meetings there were always a success.

It was like a garden in the sky and a surprise and delight for all who came to see us.

*I gathered,
and treasure,
ideas from
each of them.*

*W*hile I was living through the fast change of fashion in the office, things were moving slower at home, but definitely moving. My collecting started with early American pine, then the fascination for things French caught me. The pine was replaced with Louis XVI bergeres painted almond green, and honeyed fruitwood dining chairs with leopard velvet seats. Just as mother sent on to me some of grandmother's Chinese porcelain I met interior designer John Rieck. We worked beautifully together. A black and red lacquered table was added. A tiny hallway was papered with colorful Chinese garden scenes printed on a glossy black background. A collection of ginger jars was mounted on black lacquered brackets over a black glass mantel. My personal journey through the world of interior design had started and with a talented designer who has since become one of my best friends.

*J*ohn went on to design two offices for me. The first, at *Vogue*, was a white shell—walls, ceiling, floor. The desk was a slim, black Parsons table. The sofa and armless chairs, left over from Joseph Platt days, were upholstered in awning-striped canvas in black and white. When I was sent upstairs to *House & Garden* it seemed fitting to choose a *House & Garden* color for my new office, so John enveloped me in Mercury Grey. The walls, the ceiling, the carpeted floor, the large table desk and credenzas were all Mercury Grey. The Joseph Platt chairs, brought upstairs from *Vogue*, were recovered in a textured grey wool. A mirrored screen added sparkle, bamboo roll shades and a stack of giant baskets from Columbia added a touch of nature. It was as serene as it sounds and very conducive to work.

*I*t was my good fortune to meet many interior designers during my years as an editor of *Vogue* and editor-in-chief of *House & Garden.* Like the rolling stone I gathered, and treasure, ideas from each of them. For instance, from Billy Baldwin I learned the importance of decorating around the things you love, and about the joy of moveable furniture. He said: "After a party see how the guests have moved the chairs together for conversation and leave them that way." From Michael Taylor I learned about the utter luxury of big scale furniture, objects, plants, trees, and the allure of nature's colors and textures. From Bruce Gregga I learned about floating a few pieces of beautiful furniture in light and space. From Francois Catroux I learned about the enlivening effect of glass, mirror, and metal used deftly in a room of antiques. From David Hicks I learned about the "pow" of a patterned floor and the real glory of an

"After a party see how the guests have moved the chairs together for conversation and leave them that way."

Working with a designer of experience and taste is exhilarating.

all red room. Happily, I am still learning, keeping a sharp look around me wherever I go, and devouring the design publications with a hungry eye.

*J*ust as I was retiring from my magazine life, I moved into one of New York's handsomest old buildings. The apartment had twelve foot ceilings, heroic acanthus leaf cornices, dark herringbone floors. John Rieck had retired, too (much too young), so I asked designer Richard V. Hare to help me adapt to this glorious new space. As we stood in the living room in a golden glow—the yellow walls had already been sponged and antiqued—I felt the atmosphere called for something more exuberant than I had ever had before. I casually mentioned I had always wanted some Italian silver-leaf chairs. Richard was quick to say he had just seen a set of four in Olivieri's window. And, so my collection of painted Venetian furniture began. Each of the twenty-five pieces assembled during the last nine years entertains me, like any piece of art should. It is always more satisfying to collect a furniture style than simply to buy what is needed.

I have just moved to a smaller apartment, but with a plus: a view of

Central Park. The decoration is much the same—a yellow living room with dark herringbone floors, a study in antiqued, persimmon lacquer, a bedroom with Chinese garden scenes in pale colors. The entrance hall will be striated a hint of pink with satin white moldings. Richard Hare, a genius with color, will be there with his painter as he mixes just the right shade. His workrooms are adapting the curtains to the new windows—the yellow silk taffeta for the living room, the persimmon linen velvet for the study, and the lavendar cotton taffeta for the bedroom. His carpenter has rearranged the closets to suit my needs, added book shelves in the study, toe moldings and crown moldings in strategic places, and is preparing two sets of French doors with mirrored panes that will open and close these small spaces with some style. Richard will supervise the placement of the furniture, the pictures, and the objects so that they function well and look their best. And, he will always be on call for future additions, or subtractions, and changes-of-mind that mean progress.

*I*t is a good partnership. Working with a designer of experience and taste is exhilarating. It is a time of learning and growing. And, consulting with a professional can save you from making costly mistakes. The big reward is that it is always a joy to be at home.

Editor's Note:
Mary Jane Pool, an editor of *Vogue* Magazine and editor-in-chief of *House & Garden* 1970-1980, is a consultant to the Baker Furniture Company and Aves Advertising, Inc. She edited *Billy Baldwin Decorates* and *20th Century Decorating, Architecture and Gardens*. She is co-author of *The Angel Tree,* a book about the 18th Century Creche Collection at the Metropolitan Museum of Art, and *The Gardens of Venice* to be published by Rizzoli this year. She serves on several boards including the Decorative Arts Trust and The Isabel O'Neil Foundation for the Art of the Painted Finish.

Finding the perfect designer for creating the perfect space.

It is commonplace that our homes and offices reflect our priorities. A busy family that travels a great deal will live much differently than one that prizes the warmth and comfort of a home, or say, a couple devoted to collecting and displaying antiques or fine art. Likewise, business interiors say much about a firm's culture.

Typically, it is not until we work with an interior designer that we first intentionally articulate our priorities for our homes or business. The designer helps us to see, then enhance our priorities, making them tangible in the spaces where we live or do business.

The process of selecting a designer for a major design or furnishing project, however, can fill us with trepidation with its many complexities. So much so, that some of us would like nothing better than to throw the keys to someone else and retreat to an island in the South Pacific until the job is finished. All we need, we tell ourselves, is an interior designer who can read our mind and share every tingle of our financial anguish.

Most of us, however, prefer to participate in the process and share in the satisfaction of success. To accomplish this we need to find an interior designer who reflects our personal tastes, responds to our subtle clues, and respects our budget. Impossible as it first seems, it is possible to achieve this ideal.

The problem is not a scarcity of designers. There are scores in every region of America. The challenge of finding the one most sensitive to our personal needs (or our corporate image) can be almost as difficult as that of finding the perfect mate.

Yet the effort is surely worthwhile. Through working with a well-matched interior designer we can immeasurably increase our satisfaction in the beauty and comfort of our home.

By education and experience, interior designers understand the many practical and aesthetic aspects of creating living and working environments. They can bring resources to the project that often are otherwise unavailable. For example, where to go for the most exclusive furniture, fabrics, accessories, and all the other elements necessary for creating a truly personal environment. They know where to go for craftsmen and artisans who will manufacture custom designs that fit our needs precisely. And they are trained to take over and manage the hundreds of frustrating details of a project.

With such benefits, why don't more of us use one? Many do. Although the number of Americans who use the service of an interior designer for major design and furnishing projects is increasing every year, many still avoid asking for help. Research indicates two principal reasons why people avoid seeking professional assistance. The first and most obvious, is our fear of losing control of the budget, being intimidated into spending more than we can afford.

Our second fear is that we will lose our personal identity to someone else's vision of a picture-perfect showcase interior.

Yet perhaps the most pressing reason for not using a designer is the misunderstanding of what an interior designer can offer.

"The days of 'decorating' are over," notes Bruce Gregga, ASID, nationally acclaimed Chicago designer. "Interior design moves from the inside out. Our task is to help clients define and interpret their needs. As professionals we understand how their house should function for them."

Finding the perfect fit.

Once, the services of interior designers were only available to the privileged few, those once referred to as "the carriage trade." Three trends have converged to change this situation.

First, many more of us are now in that fortunate segment of our society termed "affluent", the segment which traditionally has turned to interior designers. Today, over 5.7 million families have household incomes of at least $75,000.

Secondly, our own education and our experiences outside the home have increased our aesthetic awareness of our environment. Today, when we travel, many of us stay in well-designed hotel rooms that raise our expectations for comfort and beauty. Likewise, the restaurants we frequent are also elaborately furnished, accessorized, and decorated. Through such experiences as these we naturally begin to desire the same or better standard for those spaces where we work, relax, or entertain.

A third trend, which triangulates the first two, is the increasing number of men and women who are graduating from design schools every year. Today you can find exceptionally skilled practitioners in virtually every major urban center.

"These professionals represent an extraordinary pool of talented, creative individuals," notes leading Chicago area designer Janet Schirn, FASID past national president of the American Society of Interior Designers (ASID). "Educated to maximize that talent and creativity, interior designers bring ideas that most clients would not have...they have tremendous exposure to the market that clients do not have, and they are more understanding of things like scale and proportion."

Among the first places to turn in the search for an interior designer is one of the professional organizations.

The American Society of Interior Designers (ASID) has a referral service in each of the 49 cities in which it's located. Their service is free, but at this time it's not entirely developed, and only includes members of ASID. When a prospective client calls ASID, the office will suggest the next three to six designers on its list, based on the particular needs of the caller. The ASID office follows-up the phone call by sending a booklet that explains the subtle details of working with a designer as well as provides tips for interviewing one.

Professional credentials remain another useful guide to selecting an interior designer. According to a study recently conducted by the magazine *1001 Home Ideas*, membership in a professional organization like ASID, International Society of Interior Designers (ISID), or the International Business Designers (IBD) is a good indication of a solid background, since members must meet tough educational and experience standards.

Nevertheless, a lack of membership in one of the "letter" organizations does not mean a lack of talent or knowledge. There are very gifted and experienced designers who feel no need for professional affiliations.

Finally, your friends and acquaintances offer another important resource for locating a compatible designer. Their successful experience and results can point you to designers who might also satisfy your needs. Indeed, like other professionals, designers find much of their new work through references from satisfied clients.

Certainly, it has been Bruce Gregga's experience. "I always ask prospective clients how they have heard of us. Usually as not, it's through someone else."

From professional organizations, friends, books such as these, you will develop a list of potentially compatible designers. Now comes the time to put faces to these names. Chances are, your list includes men and women who will present a wide range of approaches. Which one is right? To discover the answer, you will need to undertake an interview process.

Again, Gregga, "Most of us undertake a similar process for accepting new clients. When a prospective client calls, either my business manager or I will speak to him. We try to get a sense of his objectives, of what he wants. We ask clients how they would characterize their taste—do they like traditional, or are they more drawn to contemporary style. We ask about their time requirements—are they breaking ground next year, or moving into the apartment next week…"

Designers appreciate prospective clients who interview them in an orderly and businesslike manner. They are perfectly willing to answer questions about their practice.

According to another experienced professional designer, Chris Stamm,

"The prospective client should take time to shop for the right designer. Be sure to interview enough design firms and review each firm's portfolio; note whether all the work is the same; check the firm's ability to follow budgetary direction and time frame—in commercial work the time frame is particularly important."

Gregga offers a tip for evaluating the portfolio. "What makes a designer successful in his practice? Sensitivity to detail. I can't tell you how important that is in our business." For him, as for others, 'detail' goes far beyond fabrics and furnishings. "Architecture and structure must be considered." Good design affects the entire space.

Client references offer another important criterion, suggests designer Norman DeHaan, FASID, AIA. "The prospective client should know whether the project was finished on schedule, whether everything turned out the way it was supposed to, how the client felt about the budget, and whether the service was adequate to the scope of the project."

"Prospective clients should also ask about education, experience and the nature of past projects and clients," adds Janet Schirn. "They should not only ask for references, they should phone them. Prospective clients can also ask about achievements and awards in the field."

According to Greg Stratman, the interview can play a big role in finding the best fit in design assistance. "The consumer should ask questions that would indicate what sort of problem-solver the designer is. The designer should come across as being very interested in solving the client's needs. One of the most important aspects of the client/designer relationship is communications and whether or not the designer listens to what the client is saying."

Finally, there is the matter of style. Sometimes, we may not be as interested in making a personal statement of our own style preferences as we are in simply having a space that will please others. This is particularly true for commercial spaces and those areas of our home where we entertain.

Whatever style you want, you remain the key participant, notes Stamm. "It is not necessarily easy to select a design firm because it has a set style, but be sure you're compatible with that style."

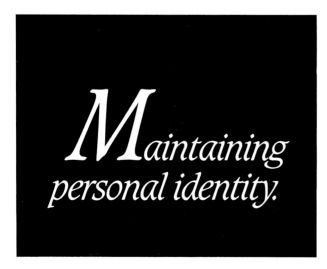

Maintaining personal identity.

Not everyone has a particular personal style which they want to feature. "There are many good clients who want a signature interior, which is entirely different from a consumer who is looking for a personal expression," observes Norman DeHaan.

Both approaches are valid, and designers respect the client who wants a designer's signature interior as well as those of us who want to feel we've made a contribution.

Notes Janet Schirn, "The trend today is not out-of-the-box design … clients are looking for something personal; a good designer does not buy everything new for a client, but takes some pieces which the client already has and builds on them."

For Schirn, this simply underscores the importance of the portfolio in making the selection.

"If there is a lot of diversity in the portfolio and if the designer makes a point of reflecting individuality in his work, then it will happen. The degree to which a client's personality and needs are represented in the job is a result of communication. Not every designer wants to do that."

As Greg Stratman points out, the designer's real role is to extend the client's possibilities. "The designer should always have the taste of the client in mind … it's the designer's job to fulfill the needs of the client and also offer alternative solutions that the client hasn't thought about. There needs to be a compromise. The designer has to take the needs of the client one step further."

*C*an we talk about money?

Some of us may actually feel that we are admitting personal inadequacy if we ask a designer how they charge or how much a project is likely to cost. Few ever reach the state where "money is not an object." Even when we enjoy very high budget ceilings we want to know what we're getting.

As Bruce Gregga notes, "Budget is a touchy subject. We talk about their understanding of how much things really cost. $5,000 for a table is not inexpensive, but it is not expensive either."

Good designers are not in business to sell merchandise, what they sell is their time and service. As professionals they have learned to keep track of every hour of their workday and also every dollar that it costs to pay themselves and their assistants, pay insurance, and other benefits, fund a retirement plan and pay for a studio or office.

It is not at all unusual for a professional designer to spend two dollars on overhead and assistance for every dollar he can pay himself. So when they charge $60 per hour for consulting time they are actually paying themselves $20 per hour. This 1-to-3 ratio of wage to hourly rate is common among many professions including lawyers, accountants and business consultants.

If a firm offers hourly rates that include all their service expenses it is a sign of professionalism. The rate may be paid directly in the form of fees or it can be paid from commissions on furniture, fabrics and other goods and services which are purchased through the design firm. There are as many variations of financial arrangements as there are client/designer agreements.

Long-lasting relationships are based on trust and candid discussions of service cost. We do not need to be timid about bringing up the subject or reviewing the status of our budget on a regular basis.

And costs certainly are controllable. As Greg Stratman states, "The designer's job is to stretch the client's budget to make every dollar count. The designer doesn't want the client to buy a $10,000 bergere and have nothing left to spend on the rest of the project. He offers the most economical solution to the client's problem."

Professional designers know that sudden 'surprises' can destroy the trust that's needed to sustain a dynamic, creative relationship. Many designers would agree with Chris Stamm when he states, "It is best for all concerned when everything is 'up front' about the scope of the project, what the fees will be, and how the client will be billed.

"The client has to realize that you pay for quality (but that doesn't mean always buying the most expensive things) and that cost is relative to satisfaction."

Cost must also be seen in light of the job, adds Gregga. "We custom design. That is, we work with different materials and sources to create a whole. Everything is related."

Nonetheless, underscores Stamm, a designer can offer important savings. "Because of the designer's better access to more furniture and related projects he can find the best quality item to fit the budget. He also saves money by avoiding the costly mistakes that some consumers make on their own."

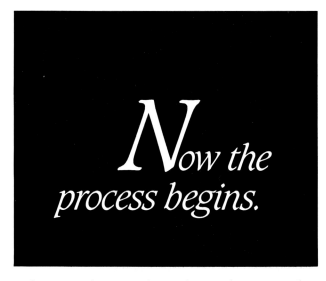

*N*ow the process begins.

When we have selected our designer the process begins. We may find that the interior designer we interviewed now wants to interview us.

For Bruce Gregga, this can be the most important meeting. "The first meeting is a 'test' to see if we can work together. Of course, the communication process has to be established and then developed.

"They interview us, we interview them. We keep the meeting to about an hour, in it we discuss their wishes, their needs, budgets, past experiences, etc. We also talk about our fee structure and time frames."

Like Gregga, Janet Schirn begins by interviewing the client to find out his tastes and dislikes. She explores in a variety of ways. "We will take a new client on some kind of a general tour of The Merchandise Mart to see what they respond to. Later, we will make definite furniture selection."

Chris Stamm also utilizes The Merchandise Mart as a resource. "We will go into The Mart and pre-select furniture pieces, carpeting, etc., and put together an entire presentation; after the presentation we take the client through The Mart to essentially 'kick the tires'...We will then have alternative selections."

This first meeting is also a good time to show our designer what we like in magazines. A tour through the pages of *Architectural Digest, HG, House Beautiful* and *1001 Home Ideas* can help us focus on things we wish we could have in our homes.

Often, it is very difficult to verbalize our tastes precisely enough to assist the designer. It is easier to find things that please and displease us.

Tearing out editorial pictures and even some ads can help us to better express ourselves to our designer. This process of selection also forces us to sort through our own impulses and study the reasons why some things work and others don't.

"Sometimes clients bring in 'pictures' of their dream house or room," comments Gregga. "This is very helpful for us; we see what they want to achieve."

Marilyn Rose, current president of the Illinois Chapter, ASID, describes the general procedure she follows with new clients:

"I go to their home. Their home tells a story of how they live by what they have chosen to surround themselves with.

"We spend a couple of hours talking about how they want to live. Some of my clients are upscaling their lives.

"I take notes on everything I see. I refer to them while I'm making a floor plan. My clients see a floor plan even before we go through The Merchandise Mart. I do a lot of leg work before I take them there.

"Some clients want a complete budget, some don't. It's surprising how many don't want to suggest a budget themselves. On commercial projects our clients are usually able to give us some budget guidelines before we begin. I prefer to know what the client really wants to spend."

For Bruce Gregga, the process is very much a partnership. "We get client approvals for everything. We make sure our client knows that questions are welcome. The more s(he) understands, the less problems will occur.

"We formalize our verbal agreement with a written contract, and new clients are asked to send us an advance payment. Then we start working on the blueprints. Of course, we review the architectural work and construction work to be done (believe me, architecture is so important! We believe in literally starting with the foundations.) Once we implement that, we then start selecting the furnishings, art, and so on."

Although each of the designers we interviewed follow somewhat different procedures, they all share some common points in their approach. Each first studies the client carefully. They all prefer clients who talk very early in the process about budget limitations, if any. Nobody we interviewed objected to working with clients who have limited budgets as long as the client has realistic goals. And each designer we talked to respects the tastes of their clients and tries to fit the design to the personal or corporate personality.

This structure provides the framework that unleashes the designer's creativity. It takes trust and openness. But the results can be electrifying, as Gregga will tell you. "The best clients allow us to do the magic and have great fun with and through the design process."

As should be clear, hiring a designer is not a sign that a person has poor taste, or is not interested in their personal surroundings. Quite the contrary. Even people with great taste and knowledge can further hone their style through working with an interior designer. As her introduction to this book so aptly illustrates, Mary Jane Pool has used designers to great effect in her home and her office while editor-in-chief of *House & Garden* and afterwards as a consultant to the furnishing industry.

The premise of this publication, *Showcase of Interior Design,* is that the careful selection of an interior designer from the broadest possible number of considerations will result in a more satisfying environment. Like any investment, hiring a designer requires some research. Although there are many to choose from, only a few will suit us precisely.

To use this book effectively, we suggest you begin by choosing three or four designers who have published their work in this book. Phone each one and talk to them about their most recent projects. Then select two or three for personal interviews in their office. Ask to see their portfolios. And ask for references. Talk to the designers about how they charge for their services. Tell them if you have a preconceived budget. Plan to have a good experience and you probably will.

Whether you have a house, an office or simply need to redo a room, with the right designer, your dreams can come true.

Dale Carol Anderson, Ltd.

Dale Carol Anderson
414 North Orleans
Suite 302
Chicago, IL 60610
(312) 661-0515

Testimonial:
"What initially impressed us about Dale was the diversity of her portfolio. As we worked with her, we began to understand the special magic she brings to each assignment. Rather than create a "Dale Carol Anderson" look, Dale really designs a "look" that is unique, yet remarkably appropriate to each client. Her sense of scale and her talent for blending furniture, fabric and finish into a statement that so fully reflects the client's own dream for their home, is a gift of immense magnitude."
      Mr. & Mrs. Harold Gershowitz
      Northbrook, IL

Philosophy:
I am equally comfortable producing sleek contemporary, as well as old world traditional interiors. Good design is synthesis; combining the needs of the client, the architecture and site, the craftsmen and artisans, all to execute the concepts developed by the client and myself. My projects are client and site specific, each is therefore unique. The only constant from project to project is that of timelessness and quality; in concept, materials and workmanship. I believe attention to detail separates a quality design project from all others and my clients clearly require this.

Client List: Private Residences: My client list includes many of Chicago's most prominent individuals; additionally I have designed residences in numerous cities throughout the U.S. and Canada.

Commercial Work: Restaurants, Boutiques and consulting for developers.

Professional Affiliations:
ASID

Education, Awards, Etc.:
Southern Illinois University–School of Design
Northwestern University
1985 Designer of the Year
Award–Residential Design

Publications:
Town & Country
Better Homes and Gardens
How To Work With An Interior Designer
      By William Turner
Northshore Magazine
Chicago Magazine
Chicago Tribune
Chicago Sun Times

Arch Associates/Stephen Guerrant, AIA

Marcia Guerrant
824 Prospect Avenue
Winnetka, IL 60093
(708) 446-7810

Testimonial:
"We have just completed a most pleasurable renovation of our home that is a wonderful showcase of Marcia's design talent. The environment that she has created for us is a fantastic expression of our taste that we never dreamed possible. We could rely on her and her staff's very professional but personal attention to our project to make us comfortable and confident in our anticipation every step of the way. Thank you Marcia!"
    Client
    Evanston, IL

Philosophy:
My personal objective is to interpret my client's taste and needs in the most creative and resourceful way. I hope that each project completed is unique from others and is a true reflection of my client's desired lifestyle.

As much as Interior Design is a creative process, it is also a service business. While making the design process an exciting and enjoyable experience for my clients, my commitment to effective communication and attention to detail insures final success and satisfaction.

Client List:
Private Residences: Chicago and North Shore areas of Illinois; Palm Springs, California; Marco Island, Florida; Lake areas of Wisconsin and Michigan; Philadelphia, Pennsylvania.

Commercial Work: Law Offices, Brokerage Offices.

Professional Affiliations:
AIA

Education, Awards, Etc.
Elmira College, Elmira, New York. Apprenticeship with several North Shore architects and interior designers. In practice as the Interior Design Group of Arch Associates since 1980.

Publications:
Better Homes and Gardens:
Remodeling Ideas
Kitchen and Bath Ideas
Decorating Ideas
Southern Living:
Creative Ideas for Living
Woman's World
Chicago Tribune

Deanna Berman Design Alternatives

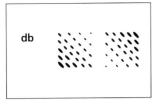

Deanna Berman
814 N. Franklin
Chicago, IL 60610
(312) 649-6611

Testimonial:
"An aesthetic bunker.

"A world in which harsh intrusion of city life are deleted, in which human sensitivites are fortified.

"A gallery where spiritually reinforcing visual art is shown and celebrated.

"A space which draws its strength from historic coliseums, and imbeds it in geometric clarity and logic of contemporary design."
Exhibit A Gallery
Chicago, IL

Philosophy:
For us a successful project is the result of an inspired reading of the initial request.

We approach design as a collaborative effort to uncover, with our clients, the unique features of each commission. This allows us to set a stage to encourage creative solutions. Special problems shape very special conclusions.

During the development of the process, we aspire to achieve a level of excellence which makes the design a statement about ingenuity and aesthetic commitment.

Our interiors draw their strength from our ability to shape the fine bones and form of a space as we determine the scale, light, color and styles of the interior design.

Client List:
Private Residences: Chicago and Chicago Suburbs, New York, California and Maryland.

Commercial Work: Mangood Corporation, InterState Steel, Pacific Brokerage Service, Giftco, Inc., Retail Shops and Showrooms, Restaurant, Art Galleries, Exhibition Consulting, Public Spaces.

Education, Awards, Etc.
University of Illinois, BA, 1959.
Practicing in Chicago since 1972.
Continuing Education at University of Chicago and Harvard University.

Publications:
Chicago Tribune
Pioneer Press
North Shore Magazine
Design Communications

Norman DeHaan Associates

Mr. Norman R. DeHaan, AIA, FASID
355 North Canal Street
Chicago, IL 60606-1207
(312) 454-0004

Mr. Carl E. Kaufman, AIA

Philosophy:
Experienced in traditional and contemporary design we bring twenty-five years of experience to the benefit of every project. An open approach to each client's individual requirements, together with our broad base of technical knowledge, brings about appropriate innovative and creative solutions. We enjoy both commercial (illustrated) and residential design.

Client List:
Private Residences: Chicago, (999, 2440, & Water Tower Place), Lake Forest & Northbrook, IL; New York, NY; & Southport, CT.

Commercial Work: Law & Real Estate Offices, Hospitals & Educational Institutions, Banks & Country Clubs.

Clients include: The Art Institute of Chicago; The University of Chicago; The Standard Club and Country Clubs: Hillcrest, Knollwood, Northmoor, Ravinia Green, Ravisloe, Twin Orchard, Westwood, MO and the renovation of the South Shore Country Club Cultural Center.

Professional Affiliations:
American Institute of Architects & the American Society of Interior Designers.

Education, Awards, Etc.
Korean Presidential Commendation, '54; Ford Foundation, '66; Chicago AIA, '66 & '88; Preservation Coalition, '85; Institute of Store Planners, '70 & '72; Executive Offices Design, '77; ASID National Design of Distinction, '85; Art Institute, Architecture Interiors Exhibit, '89.

Mr. DeHaan has served as National President of ASID, President of the Chicago Chapter of the AIA, National Chairman of the AIA Interiors Committee. He currently serves as President-Elect of the International Federation of Interior Designers in Amsterdam, Vice President of the Bright New City Foundation, and the steering committee of Sculpture Chicago. Additional information is available in Who's Who in America and Who's Who in the World.

Busch|Noha|Williams Interior Design

F. Marie Busch, ASID (middle),
Andrew F. Noha, ISID (right),
Bruce A. Williams, ISID (left)
1735 W. Fletcher
Chicago, IL 60657
(312) 549-1414

Busch|Noha|Williams Interior Design

Philosophy:
Creative, flexible and enthusiastic; we strive to develop a design that combines our clients' unique set of needs and desires.

We love the intricacies of interior design and pay a great deal of attention to detail, color, fabrics and accessories.

Developing a strong set of design precepts enables us to create unusual, dramatic, comfortable and timeless design solutions.

We feel our clients appreciate the extra thought that goes into each project.

Client List:
Private Residences: Chicago, North Shore and all suburban areas. Atlanta, Hilton Head, Florida, Scottsdale, San Diego and London, England.

Commercial Work: Executive Offices, Country Clubs, Restaurants and small Hotels.

Professional Affiliations:
ASID, ISID

Education, Awards, Etc.:
F. Marie Busch, ASID; Miss Busch studied Design and Fine Arts at Stephens College and the Harrington Institute of Interior Design.

Andrew F. Noha, ISID; Mr. Noha studied Business and Design at Drake University.

Bruce A. Williams, ISID; Mr. Williams studied History of Art and Architecture at the University of Illinois at Chicago Circle and also Mr. Williams studied Design at the Harrington Institute of Interior Design.

All three members of the firm have been practicing interior design in the Chicago area since 1978.

Aside from client work they are active participants in Chicago area Designer Showcase Houses and Vignettes for charitable fundraisers.

In 1988 they were awarded a special recognition award from Chicago Design Sources and The Merchandise Mart for excellence in Interior Design.

In 1989 they were selected by *House Beautiful* as one of the top ten Design Showcase House rooms in the country.

Camwilde Interiors

Ann L. Wildblood,
Associate Member ASID
522 Chestnut St.
Hinsdale, IL 60521
(708) 887-8828

Testimonial:
"Our home today better expresses the personality of our family than if we had done it ourselves. Our home is now our 'get-away'. Through a unique use of cool colors and elements of wit and whimsy, they were able to tap our imagination. Camwilde didn't follow our taste, they led it."

> Tom and Karen Terry
> Chicago North Shore

"Commuting between New York and Chicago limited the time we could spend on our new Chicago residence. We needed someone who was efficient and could give us something out of the ordinary. I put my trust in Camwilde. Their ability to envision the 'whole' was invaluable. The results are beyond our expectations."

> Warren and Lynn Flick
> Chicago Gold Coast

Philosophy:
Rather than a "look", we strive to achieve a total "feeling"—an interplay of visual and other sensory elements, while remaining true to the architectural character of the space. We are able to stretch a client's sense of design through creative uses of color, texture, and art, to add dimension to the space.

Our goal is to develop a design solution, which will complement the client's taste, as well as their lifestyle. We know we have succeeded when the client enjoys the design process as well as the final results.

Client List:

Private Residences: Chicago's Gold Coast and North Shore, Oak Brook, and other select areas in Chicago; Los Angeles; Boca Raton; Atlanta.

Commercial Work: Corporate Executive Offices, and Private Professional Offices.

Education, Awards, Etc.
Ms. Wildblood received a BA degree from the University of Iowa in 1969, an interior design degree from the College of DuPage in 1980, and a Masters of Management degree in 1985 from Northwestern University Kellogg School of Management. Through her participation in several Chicago-area showcase projects, she has received recognition for her design creativity.

Publications:
Chicago Tribune
Crain's Chicago Business
Chicago Sun Times

Laurie Cowall

1720 North LaSalle Drive
Unit 1
Chicago, IL 60614
(312) 280-8044

Client List:
Private Residences: North Shore, Chicago, Barrington and Rockford, Illinois; Indianapolis, Indiana; Beverly Hills, San Diego and Portola Valley in California; Aspen, Colorado; Phoenix, Arizona.

Commercial Work: Food Processing Company, Law Offices, Retail Store, Brokerage House, Executive Offices and Corporate Apartment.

Professional Affiliations:
ISID

Education, Awards, Etc.:
Bradley University
Harrington Institute, 1970
Chicago Lighting Institute, 1970

Publications:
Chicago Tribune
Chicago Tribune, Sunday Magazine
Chicago Sun Times
Home Furnishings Ideas
Skyline
Metropolitan Home
Ebony
Better Homes and Gardens
Decorating
Furnishings and Decorating Ideas

Testimonial:
"Working with Laurie is like sharing time with a good friend. His casual, relaxed approach to design put us at ease immediately. Our desire was to make our new home sophisticated, yet comfortable enough for our six-year-old and her playmates. Laurie has accomplished our goals and more. From the beginning, I knew that I wanted to be totally involved in the design process. Laurie welcomed me on our shopping excursions! I soon realized that forming a close personal relationship with his clients is as rewarding and important to him as designing a beautiful environment."
 Deborah Dockendorf
 Chicago, IL

Philosophy:
Collaborating with my clients and developing a friendship makes the design process an enjoyable experience with the end result being special and unique. Extensive time is shared developing and upgrading the client's expectations by exposing them to a multitude of possibilities. Through this joint effort, we create a practical interior of fine quality and excellent design.

Larry N. Deutsch Interiors, Ltd.

Larry N. Deutsch, ASID
325 West Huron Street
Suite 500
Chicago, IL 60610
(312) 649-1244

Client List:
Private Residences: Chicago's Gold Coast and North Shore; Manhattan and select areas of the East Coast; North and South Florida (including the Palm Beach area); Beverly Hills, Palm Springs, San Francisco and around California; other cities across the United States.

Commercial Work: Financial Services and Insurance Offices, Retirement and Geriatric Centers, Private Yachts.

Professional Affiliations:
ASID

Education, Awards, Etc.:
University of Arizona, BFA, 1963; Second Place, The National Barcalounger Competition, Best Design of a Multi-Purpose Room, 1977; Outstanding Achievement in Design, The Merchandise Mart, Chicago, 1986; Chairman, National ASID Conference, Chicago, 1984; Business Chairman, National ASID Conference, Los Angeles, 1986; Ex-officio Member, National ASID Industry Foundation Steering Committee; Past involvement as Board Member, Vice President and Education Committee Chairman of the Illinois Chapter of the ASID.

Publications:
Architectural Digest
House & Garden
House Beautiful
Better Homes and Gardens
Chicago Tribune
The Designer

Testimonial:
Larry's designs are creative and appropriate solutions to our needs. He treats each project with careful attention to detail, without losing sight of our goals. His elegant style and special touch have created unique living environments for us.
   Mrs. Audrey Altounian
   Lake Forest, IL
   Ponte Vedra, FL

Philosophy:
The key to success is a commitment to a set of principles based on achieving the highest level of professionalism. We design for the client's lifestyle and interpret those lifestyle needs selectively through fine art and furnishings. We work closely with in-house architects in order to maximize the structural elements of a space. We believe that positive client communications, creative solutions, and good business practices result in elegant design.

DeVos Residence, Holland, MI

Gerald R. Ford Presidential Museum

DuBAY & MAIRE, LTD.

Daniel DuBay
Gregory Maire
111 East Chestnut Street
Chicago, IL 60611
(312) 951-6222

Philosophy:
We strive to bring forth specialized design solutions that address the needs of today's fast paced society, while creating dramatic effects of an individual nature which are timeless. The innovative use of luxurious, classic materials, alone and in combination, has become a trademark.

We believe that our client's lifestyles and needs should be enhanced by good design and architecture. Our responsibility is to help our clients interpret their aspirations through fine objects, art and antiques.

For example, as shown below, maintaining a balance between restoration of a richly detailed vintage Gold Coast residence and updating it for family living was the primary focus of both client and the designers. The client wished to incorporate a growing collection of fine antique English and French furnishings and accessories without creating a museum-like ambiance. The outcome is clear: An interior which is a superb backdrop for formal gatherings yet accommodates the lifestyles of a busy professional couple and their family.

Client List:
Private Residences: Chicago's Gold Coast and North Shore, New York, Connecticut, Washington, D.C., Palm Springs and other California cities. Commercial work includes several Chicago Law Offices, Major Developments, i.e. extensive involvement with JMB/Urban Investment & Development, on the residential complex at 900 North Michigan Avenue; BCE Development and Sudler-Marling, on the residential complex at 700 North Michigan Avenue; and Olympia & York, on a model residence at Olympia Centre.

Education, Awards, Etc.:
Mr. DuBay studied design at Drake University and has been a practicing professional since 1972. Mr. Maire joined him in 1982, bringing to the firm his Masters training in architecture from Harvard University. Aside from their professional practice, both are involved in civic and charitable activities.

Publications:
Chicago Tribune
Chicago Sun Times
Chicago Magazine
How to Work With an Interior Designer
by William Turner
Interior Design Magazine
(Fall 1989)

Fernandez & George, Inc.

Agustin Fernandez

Robert George, ASID

230 West Huron
Chicago, IL 60611
(312) 649-5744

Fernández & George
Interior Design

Testimonial:
"We are thrilled with our home after working with Fernandez & George. Having gone through four other nationally known designers, it wasn't until Agustin and Robert came on board that this difficult space became workable, livable, and extraordinarily beautiful."

Philosophy:
Urban. Baroque. Slick. Opulent. Disciplined. Romantic. Technological. Edit, Edit, Edit... Details, Details, Details...

Client List:
Private Residences:
Chicago, New York, Los Angeles, Coral Gables, Mexico City and Caracas.

Commercial Work:
Chicago: Legal Offices, Corporate Headquarters, Boutiques, Restaurants. New York: Real Estate Developers, Corporate Headquarters.

Education, Awards, Etc.:
Robert George, ASID: Ray Vogue School of Design; Harrington Institute, Board of Directors ASID.
   Agustin Fernandez: American School of Madrid, Spain; Wittenberg University; Parsons School of Design, New York; and Harvard University

Publications:
House & Garden
Metropolitan Home
New York Magazine
Decoration
Casa Vogue
Chicago Tribune
Chicago Sun Times
New York Times

Architecture by Stanley Tigerman

Frosolone Interiors Ltd.

William A. Frosolone
400 North Wells, Suite 344
Chicago, IL 60610
(312) 828-1118

Philosophy:

Through creative use of space, interiors can reflect mood, philosophy, or marketing strategy. Interiors can suggest success, elegance, comfort, purposefulness and trust. The key to the success of any one interior and its designers is to clearly define its purpose and reflect its ownership or market. A designer should interpret and communicate client lifestyle, not his personal design statement.

Client List:

Private Residences: Chicago's Gold Coast, Manhattan, La Jolla, Boca Raton, Palm Beach.

Commercial Work: Hospitals, Hotels, Restaurants, Health Clubs, Corporate Offices in various national locations, Retail Spaces.

Education, Awards, Etc.

Mr. Frosolone is an alumnus of Chicago's Harrington Institute of Interior Design and began his firm in 1973. In addition to his client work, he enjoys guest lecturing for interior design seminars.

Publications:

Chicago Tribune
Chicago Sun Times
Builder Magazine
Better Homes and Gardens

Testimonial:

"Bill has the most complete understanding of interior design. He captures the personality and style of the client in his designs. He has designed all of my residences from Manhattan to Chicago, my Ft. Lauderdale apartment to my Florida Keys retreat, to my ocean view home in Greece.

"With each assignment, Bill created unique interiors. His designs range from the most elegant to gracious casualness, reflecting my lifestyle in each home."

Evangeline Gouletas-Carey
New York, NY

Barbara M. Fullerton Interiors Ltd.

Barbara M. Fullerton ISID
17700 West Capitol Drive
Brookfield, WI 53005
(414) 781-0140

Client List:
Private Residences: Wisconsin, Kentucky, Ohio, Connecticut, and Florida.

Commercial Work: Chenequa Country Club, Oconomowoc Lake Club, Corporate Headquarters, Retirement Centers, Medical Facilities, Law Offices, Restaurants in Milwaukee and Boston.

Professional Affiliations:
ISID, Allied Member ASID, Board of Directors, Wisconsin Chapter of ISID, Historic Preservation Committee, ISID

Education, Awards, Etc.
Degree and Certification, University of Cincinnati, College of Design, Art and Architecture. Inchbald School of Design, London. Thirty years study of 18th Century American Architecture, 1st Place ASID Trade Fair 1984, Guest lecturer Milwaukee Area Technical College.

Publications:
The Milwaukee Journal
The Milwaukee Sentinel
The Waukesha Freeman
Professional Builder
Inland Shores
Soon to be published, *Designing and Building an 18th Century Style Fireplace*

Testimonial:
"Barbara is recognized in the Midwest as a leading authority on 18th Century American architecture and interiors. Working in this period, her knowledge is applied through millwork design, masonry details and color. This combination of skills, along with her sense of style and comfort, produces rooms that are truly warm and unique."
  Ronald P. Siepmann
  Land Developer/Builder
  Brookfield, WI

Philosophy:
My responsibility to my clients is to assess their needs and lifestyles, never urging them away from the style with which they are comfortable, yet asking them to expand on their preference. The best design solutions result in always considering every element in a space and a commitment to paying attention to detail.

Paul Granata Interiors

Paul Granata
330 West Diversey Parkway
Suite 503
Chicago, IL 60657
(312) 883-1930

Testimonial:
"I've known Paul from pre-both our Chicago design days. He is a terrific young talent with a great people touch, abundant energy and excellent attention to detail. Working with Paul should be a genuine pleasure."
    Holly Hunt
    Holly Hunt LTD.

Philosophy:
A room should be a delight to the senses whether it be the combination of lighting, textures, furnishing or forms. The space should fascinate the eye and make you feel good about being a part of the environment.

My pleasure is to create an emotion upon entering a room.

Whether it quickens the heartbeat or quiets the spirit, an interior should evoke a response.

My clients are an integral part of the creative process. I strive to interpret their wishes with enthusiasm, professionalism and sensitivity.

Client List:
Private Residences: In Chicago's Gold Coast, North Shore, and other surrounding areas. South Florida (including Boca Raton) and East coast (including Hilton Head, North Carolina).

Education, Awards, Etc.:
Paul Granata created an important vignette that was sponsored by Tiffany Jewelers for the International Garden and Flower Exhibition, 1988.
He is a graduate of the University of Illinois and Harrington Institute of Interior Design. Paul has taken miscellaneous classes at Northwestern and DePaul Universities and is a permanent student of the lessons of life.

Publications:
Chicago Tribune
Metropolitan Home Magazine
Skyline Newspaper

Lynn Graves Associates, Ltd.

Lynn F. Graves
731 West 18th Street, Suite #11
Chicago, IL 60616
(312) 243-1037

Testimonial:
"When we hired Lynn Graves Associates to redo our corporate offices I was confident that her firm would do a competent job. Her work for us transcends competence! Our environment is full of magic and delight. I can see the results of her work in the attitude of my employees."
> Mr. Rick Van Horne, President
> Corrugated Supplies
> Corporation

Philosophy:
We particularly enjoy working with the structure and architecture of the buildings whenever possible. This enables us to unify the concept of the interior space with its architectural elements. It is important for us to appreciate our clients' concept of themselves—how they want to work, project themselves, and create in their environment. The result is a series of spaces that answers the client's needs and comfort, while being surrounded by beautiful finishes, furnishings and objects.

Client List:
Private Residences: The Gold Coast, North Shore and select areas in Chicago and around Illinois.

Commercial Work: Corporate Offices, Financial Facilities, Developments in the River North Gallery Districts, and various Medical Facilities in the greater Chicago area.

Education, Awards, Etc.:
University of Cincinnati-Bachelor of Science, 1976 Ohio State University, Fine Arts, 1971; Professional Practice Program of U.C.

Bruce Gregga Interiors, Inc.

Bruce Gregga
1203 North State Parkway
Chicago, IL 60610
(312) 787-0017

Testimonial:
"When he did our apartment, we gave him total freedom, and he produced comfort, tranquility, and beauty. He devised the space like an architect…Thoughtful and concerned for what makes people completely at ease in their surroundings…"
  Mrs. Henry Paschen
  Chicago, IL

Philosophy:
Interiors have to work for the people who will live in them. They should be an extension of a person's self, a reflection of his or her lifestyle, not the designer's "Design Statement."

Client List:
Private Residences: Victor Skrebneski, Chicago, IL; Mr. and Mrs. Henry Paschen, Chicago, IL; Martha's Vineyard, MA, and New York City; Mr. and Mrs. Lewis Manilow, Chicago, IL and various other residences in Chicago, IL; Palm Beach, FL; Palm Springs, Beverly Hills, CA; and New York City.

Commercial Work: Standard Club of Chicago; Whitehall Hotel, Chicago, IL; Ultimo, Chicago, IL; several McDonalds Restaurants in Indiana and vicinity.

Professional Affiliations:
ASID

Education, Awards, Etc.:
1983 Residential Design Excellence Award from the Chicago Design Sources & Merchandise Mart. 1987 Interior Design Magazine Hall of Fame Award. 1988 Dean of Design Award Chicago Design Sources & Merchandise Mart. 1988 Who's Who In Interior Design.

Publications:
Architectural Digest: 9/78, 12/78, 5/80, 12/80, 9/82, 2/83, 10/84, 5/85, 10/87, 7/88, 3/89, 7/89, 10/89.
House & Garden: 2/75, 9/85.
Interior Design Magazine: 8/85, 12/87 (Hall of Fame Issue)

Handman Associates

Shelly Handman
1440 N. Dayton
Chicago, IL 60622
(312) 951-8456

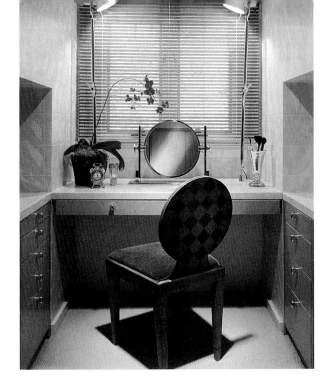

Philosophy:
A successful project is when our clients feel that their home has evolved as a result of our collaboration. Their personality is what shapes the project; we, the designers, bring the balance, restraint and life to it. Together we create a uniquely styled space.

Client List:
Private Residences: Chicago's Gold Coast and North Shore; Atlanta, Georgia; Maimi and Boca Raton, Florida; Laguna Beach and Malibu, California.

Commercial Work: Law Offices, Optical Shops, Residential Complex (including Health Club, Restaurant and Commissary.)

Professional Affiliations:
ASID—Allied Member

Education, Awards, Etc.
After graduating as an art major from Northern Illinois University, Shelly Handman finished his formal design training at Harrington Institute of Interior Design.

Publications:
Chicago Tribune
Chicago Sun Times
Kitchen and Bath
Apartment Life
Decorating
Great American Decorating

Laura Barnett Henderson Inc.

Laura Henderson, ISID
708 Church Street,
Suite 252
Evanston, IL 60201
(708) 864-4150

Testimonial:
"Laura is an exceptional talent. She is incredibly creative with an impeccable sense of beauty and design. We have worked on a variety of projects with her, from designing office space to decorating our home. Her sense of style is complex and out of the ordinary, yet, she never loses the human touch. Laura is a delight to work with, she listens well and translates our wishes into reality."
    Dr. and Mrs. Dennis Grygotis

Philosophy:
Working with interior design and architecture allows us to completely change an interior environment to one that is visually pleasing to the people living or working there. It's exciting to watch the changes, in the space as well as the owner's response to the space. Concentrating on the planning stages enables one to attack the "problem" at its source. Use of beautiful color, fabrics and textures then can enhance the room and allow the client's personality to shine through.

Creativity, expertise, attention to quality and detail. Combine these with a high level of professionalism and a commitment to excellence, then you've achieved a successful design.

Client List:
Private Residences: Chicagoland, including the Gold Coast, Lincoln Park, DePaul, North Shore, Western suburbs. Summer residences, Michigan & Wisconsin. San Diego & Los Angeles, CA.

Commercial Work: Law Offices: One Magnificent Mile, Quaker Tower. President's Suite: Museum of Science & Industry. Restaurant: Lincoln Park. Retail Stores: suburban locations and Lexington, KY. Doctor's Offices: Old Orchard, downtown Chicago. Marketing Firms: four, downtown Chicago.

Professional Affiliations:
ISID

Education, Awards, Etc.:
Interior Architecture & Design, Chicago Academy of Fine Arts.
Park Ridge Youth Campus Designer Showhouses: '86, '87, '88.
Speaker and vignette designer, Merchandise Mart: '86, '87, '88, '89.
Winner 1988 SPECIAL DESIGN RECOGNITION AWARD from Chicago Design Sources & The Merchandise Mart.
Charity design projects: Make A Wish Chicago, Orchard Village for the mentally handicapped.
Vice President, Board Member, Committee Chairman: International Society of Interior Designers.

Publications:
Chicago Tribune, Chicago Sun Times, North Shore Magazine, Better Homes and Gardens Decorating, Better Homes and Gardens, Pioneer Press, Paddock Publications, Architectural Digest's Design Decision.

HSP/Ltd.-Seglin Associates

David A. Seglin
1725 West North Ave.
Chicago, IL 60622
(312) 252-7100

Philosophy:
Ours is a growing architectural
practice that maintains a strong
commitment to high quality design
and construction. The scope of the
firm's work includes renovations,
new construction and interior design. Providing a complete range of
architectural and interior design
services, we have completed both
residential and commercial projects
for developers, corporations
and private clients.

Client List:
Private Residences: The Metal-
Works Loft Condominiums, Chi-
cago; Grimes Residence, Chicago;
Olympia Center Condominium, Chi-
cago; House Addition and Renova-
tion, Clarendon Hills, Illinois; 2400
N. Lakeview Condominium, Chi-
cago; Historic Home Addition and
Renovation, Evanston, Illinois.

Commercial Work: Randolph Office
Supply, Chicago; Corporate Offices
for Geraghty and Miller Inc.,
Chicago.

Professional Affiliations:
AIA

Education, Awards, Etc.:
Lake Forest College, BA 1977
Princeton University, Master of
Architecture 1981.

Mr. Aluise graduated with High Honors from the International Academy of Merchandising and Design, Chicago; recipient of three designer debut awards including first place for rendering techniques, second place for Contract Design and third place for Residential Interior Design; served as treasurer of the Interior Design Club.

Mr. Brischetto and Mr. Aluise employ an imaginative use of Gestalt Design theory to client's design problems that result in a fresh architectural approach in solving space planning needs.

Publications:
The Designer
Interior Design
Residential Interiors
Chicago Tribune
Chicago Sun Times
The Daily Southtown Economist
The Oak Leaves
The Domino Page

Janie Petkus Interiors

Janie Petkus, ISID
42 Village Place
Hinsdale, IL 60521
(708) 325-3242

Testimonial:
"Janie *listens* to her clients, and works within the parameters of style and budget that they dictate. She has a terrific eye for color, and her enthusiasm for each project makes it a pleasure to work with her."

Mrs. Jim Porter
Hinsdale, IL

Philosophy:
A good client-designer relationship is built on mutual trust. I believe my client's homes or offices should be a reflection of *their* personality and style and not mine. I enjoy working with them to combine color, fabrics, artwork, antiques and furnishings so that they feel comfortable as well as proud of the finished product.

Client List:
Private Residences: Hinsdale, Oak Brook, North Shore and select areas of Chicago; Atlanta; Sea Island, Georgia; Charleston, South Carolina; Houston, Texas; and other cities across the United States.

Commercial Work: Professional Offices—Medical, Dental, Legal and Financial Services.

Professional Affiliations:
ISID

Education, Awards, Etc.:
A graduate of the University of Illinois, Champaign-Urbana, Ms. Petkus taught Interior Design at Harper Jr. College and the College of DuPage before opening her own Interior Design business in 1978. ISID National Historic Presentation Award for work done with Hinsdale Historical Society 1989; Listed in Barron's Who's Who in Interior De-

sign 1989; Represented the Woolite Company as National Design Consultant 1987-1988; Design Consultant for "Today Show" segment aired December 9, 1986; Served on board for the Illinois Chapter of ISID.

Publications:
Chicago Tribune
Chicago Sun Times
Better Homes and Gardens
Home Magazine
Family Circle
Better Homes and Gardens
    Decorating
Woman's World
Country Living
Victoria

Freiwald/Associates, Inc.

Richard J. Freiwald
920 N. Franklin St.
Suite 305
Chicago, IL 60610
(312) 642-6890

Testimonial:
"Dick's strong educational and Fine Arts background made the process of detailing our home from conception through construction and on to final decorating both a learning experience and a pleasure. He advised us on all facets of the project; pointing out alternatives and solutions to the on-site problems during construction, always keeping in mind the final goal. Both my husband and I learned a great deal in the process, with the result being a home we feel is both beautiful and livable. I keep wanting to move again (this is our third home Dick has helped us with) in order to create another house with 'that Freiwald Touch'."
　　A Client
　　Chicago, IL

Philosophy:
At Freiwald Associates, Inc., we pride ourselves on incorporating our client's personality and needs into the design process from the beginning. Whether working together on a contemporary media room, period law office or with cherished antiques, our design flows with the appropriate style to realize our clients' aspirations for fine living. Our relationships with several clients, extending through the years and on multiple projects, reflect the design staffs' foremost commitment to service. This attention to service, whether to our client, the architect, contractor, or the trade person, is the factor that helps Freiwald Associates, Inc. achieve a definitive look through well-constructed design, quality materials, furnishings and fine art.

Client List:
Residential, Corporate, Legal Offices and Medical Facilities in: Chicago & Metropolitan Area, Northern Suburbs of Detroit, Southern Florida, California, Vale, Aspen, Houston, Memphis, Montreal and London, England.

Education:
Central Michigan University, Fine Arts & Education, B.A.
Wayne State University, Graduate School

Publications:
Better Homes & Gardens
Home
House Beautiful
Chicago Tribune
Chicago Sun Times
The Detroit News

John Robert Wiltgen Design, Inc.

John Robert Wiltgen
300 W. Grand Avenue
Suite 306
Chicago, IL 60610
(312) 744-1151

Testimonial:

"Can we talk!?" John Robert Wiltgen is a young man on the rise. Our professional relationship began four years ago in a design showroom, as he became my client. His creativity, intelligence and loyalty represent a special human being in every sense of the word. John's charm and wit extend beyond a professional level, into a sincere, warm friendship with a commitment to you, as an individual.

"'So to speak, to know him is to love him.' His humanness is apparent socially and in his design practice; as I now have become part of both of his worlds.

"A smile always appears on his face. Never a complaint is uttered, laughter or nice words are always heard. His positive attitude is his greatest attribute. So happy our paths did cross, John Robert Wiltgen. Good luck and good health."

Maureen L. Netsky
Rozmallin Showroom

Philosophy:

Today everything is too expensive to get caught up in trends. Our interior design concepts are meticulously planned resulting in environments that are aesthetically rich, totally functional, and enduringly timeless. The key to the success of our commissions is our ability to interpret the ideas, dreams, and lifestyles of our clients and translate that into their surroundings.

"If I had to use one word to describe our work, I'd say it was 'appropriate'; appropriate to the architecture of the space, its function, and most importantly, to our clients."

Client List:

Private Residences: Private Gold Coast residences including co-ops at 179 E. Lake Shore Drive, 999 E. Lake Shore Drive, 3920 N. Lake Shore Drive; luxury condominiums including 20 E. Cedar Drive, 1366 N. Dearborn, 1000 N. Lake Shore Plaza, Water Tower Place, One Mag Mile; Lincoln Park and DePaul rowhouses; and, suburban estates including Wilmette, Northbrook, Highland Park, Lake Forest, Hinsdale, Oak Brook, Barrington Hills, and Lake Geneva. Out of state residences including New York, Connecticut and California.

Commercial Work: Commercial work including model apartments for four National Landmark Buildings; total interior design concept for 1212 S. Michigan Avenue; three model apartments for Parkway Place, Atlanta, Georgia; three model homes for Hardstadt Todd Construction, Minneapolis, Minnesota. Private rooms, corridors, Surgeon's Administrative Offices and Doctor's Lounge for Grant Hospital; Jefferson Park Professional Building; and more including executive offices, retail stores, banks, and health clubs.

John Robert Wiltgen Design, Inc.

Professional Affiliations:
International Society of Interior Designers; represented by Decorator Previews Chicago; member Landmark Preservation Council of Illinois; board member Better Boys Foundation and chairman for their 1989 10th Annual Celebrity Auction

Education, Awards, Etc.:
Ray Vogue College of Design
Harvard University, Graduate School of Design

Publications:
PM Magazine, North Shore Magazine, Avenue M Magazine, Chicago Tribune, Chicago Sun Times, Daily and Sunday Herald, Paddock Publications, Inc., Barron's Who's Who in Interior Design

Carol R. Knott Interior Design

Carol R. Knott
430 Green Bay Road
Kenilworth, IL 60043
(708) 256-6676

Testimonial:
"Only once before in my experience with Harry Hinson did I see a room in which a designer understood what we mean by pretty.

"You have outdone that original room by half—and more. We are very much in your debt."
Philip McKinney
Vice President
Hinson & Company
New York

Philosophy:
My responsibility is to interpret the client's wishes and desires. Through open communication, we first identify a concept of how they would like to live. I then strive to implement the design process in a professional manner. I know I have done my part when the client feels thrilled with the end result and I feel personally rewarded.

Client List:
Private Residences: Apartments; Vacation Homes: Chicago's Gold Coast; Lincoln Park area; North Shore; Barrington; Hinsdale; Wisconsin; Michigan; Greenwich, CT; Staunton, VA; New Jersey; West Virginia; Hilton Head, SC; Ft. Lauderdale, FL; Naples, FL; San Francisco, CA; Phoenix, AZ; Canada and Portugal.

Commercial Work: Executive Offices and Medical Suites.

Professional Affiliations:
1966-present Professional Member American Society of Interior Designers, Illinois Chapter (Board of Directors-2 years); Chicago Designer Club

Education, Awards, Etc.
Northwestern University, 1966; The Academy of Lighting Arts, 1966; Interior Design 1978 Advisory Panel; American Institute of Interior Designers, 1970; Who's Who of American Women; Who's Who in the Midwest; Who's Who in Interior Design; Residential Interior Design Excellence Award, The Merchandise Mart/Chicago Design Sources, 1989.

Publications:
Chicago Tribune
Chicago Sun Times
The Pioneer Press
House & Garden
Woman's World
Pierre Deux's French Country
1981 Better Homes and Gardens Decorating Book

Lili Kray, FISID

Lili Kray, FISID
1625 Merchandise Mart
Chicago, IL 60654
and
4300 Ponchartrain
New Buffalo, MI 49117
(616) 469-4161

Testimonial:
"When we first viewed the model that Lili Kray had designed, we knew that she was the one to design our weekend retreat. Her style and panache were just what was required. Lili created an environment that reflected our taste and preferences. It is exactly what we had hoped for in a second home. We think of Lili gratefully each time we visit and are renewed."
     Pat and John Gorman
     Gorman Publishing,
     Chicago, IL

Philosophy:
To evolve and develop all potential aspects of the design for each individual project...to include the "attitudes" of person and personality, whether residential or commercial...to envelop the client's desires and needs...to create an interior that enriches those within its realm.

Client List:
Private Residences: Chicago's Gold Coast, North Shore, Barrington, Palos Park; Beverly Shores, Indiana; Scottsdale, Arizona; La Jolla, California; Palm Beach, Singer Island, East-Pointe Country Club, Florida; Vail, Colorado and select areas of the East Coast.

Commercial Work: Law Offices; Classic Automobile Gallery; Stores; Boutiques; Model Homes and Apartments, Chicago; New Buffalo, Michigan and in other cities across the United States.

Professional Affiliations:
ISID

Education, Awards, Etc.:
Ray Vogue; Art Institute; Fellowship, International Society of Interior Designers; International ISID Vice President, Membership Development ISID; Past National Council for Interior Design Qualification Board Member (NCIDQ); Past Chairman of the Board, President, International Representative for the Illinois Chapter, ISID.

Publications:
Chicago Tribune
Chicago Sun Times
South Bend Magazine and various Chicagoland publications

Photo Credit:
Photographer: Barry J. Kray

Winnie Levin Interiors, Ltd.

Winifred Levin
614 Laurel
Highland Park, IL 60035
(708) 433-7585

Testimonial:
"Winnie took a creative approach toward designing a comfortable home to suit our lifestyle. She paid careful attention to detail, always keeping in mind our specific wishes and needs. Winnie's artistic expertise enabled us to successfully achieve the kind of warm and sophisticated environment we desired."
    Client
    Chicago, IL

Philosophy:
Whether contemporary or traditional, I attempt to fully understand the needs of my clients. I enjoy the challenge of creating a unique and exciting atmosphere, capturing one's spirit and individuality. My idea of a successful project is the transformation of space into the reflection of its inhabiters.

Client List:
Private Residences: The Gold Coast, Chicago and surrounding suburbs; Lake Geneva, Wisconsin; Palm Beach and Boca Raton, Florida; Toronto, Canada.

Commercial Work: Executive Offices, Board of Trade, Chicago; Corporate Residence, Palm Beach, Florida; Doctor's Offices; Law Offices; Condominium Lobbies.

Education, Awards, Etc.
Ms. Levin studied design at Indiana University and has been practicing in the Chicago area since 1977. Prior to that time, she was a professional artist exhibiting in juried shows and galleries throughout the Midwest.

Publications:
Chicago Sun Times

Susan Kroeger, Ltd.

Susan Kroeger
253 Franklin Rd.
Glencoe, IL 60022
(708) 835-5262

Testimonial:
"Our home is so rich and satisfying. Susan has made it our special place—when we return after a trip, we are always delighted that this is our home."
    Client
    Chicago, IL

"Susan has the talent to see new relationships of space where they didn't exist before. She delights in turning ordinary rooms into exciting environments."
    Client
    Chicago, IL

Philosophy:
Since my involvement in the industry in 1972, I have maintained that an interior designer's responsibility is to understand the client's dream and make it a reality. A room or home should reflect and enhance its owner. All clients have a natural right to elegance, style and comfort. When this has been achieved, we know we have done our part.

Client List:
Private residences in the North Shore, Gold Coast and other select areas around Chicago; California; Arizona; Wisconsin; Indiana; Florida; Rhode Island and New York City.

Affiliations:
Affiliate Member, ASID

Education, Awards, Etc.:
Maryville College, St. Louis, MO, Bachelor of Arts
Postgraduate Studies, St. Louis University, MO
Participation in Showcase Houses—Infant Welfare Society, Park Ridge, ORT, and others.

Publications:
North Shore Magazine
Chicago Sun Times
Chicago Tribune
Better Homes & Garden's Special Editions
Chicago Magazine

Lise Lawson Interior Design, Ltd.

Lise Lawson, ASID, IBD
6420 N. Lake Drive
Milwaukee, WI 53217
(414) 351-6334

Testimonial:
"Through Lise's experience with specialty providers and her contacts with skilled craftsmen and artists, she was able to present us with unique and wonderful alternatives from which to choose.

"Each room in our home has its own special ambiance and yet each flows beautifully into another."
Client
Milwaukee, WI

Philosophy:
The potential for design excellence exists in every interior when communication skills and design skills merge. Because our work encompasses residential projects to large commercial office interiors, we have had to learn to respond to the needs of a diverse clientele. A design group that offers services to varying market segments can only be successful by listening to the client's needs, honoring the client's budget and schedule, and keeping alert to the creative use of products and technologies.

Client List:
Private Residences: Private Residences in Milwaukee, Madison, Door County, Chicago, Washington, DC.

Commercial Work: Corporate Offices, Health Care Facilities, Banks, Restaurants, Senior Citizen Facilities, Law Offices.

Professional Affiliations:
ASID, President Wisconsin Chapter of ASID (1989), IBD, Council Member (National Director 1986-1988), NCIDQ (National Council of Interior Design Qualification)

Education, Awards, Etc.:
BA History of Art, University of Michigan; BA Interior Design, Mt. Vernon College, Washington, DC; contract and residential design awards (Wisconsin)

Publications:
Milwaukee Journal
Milwaukee Sentinel
Milwaukee Magazine
Wisconsin Architect
Better Homes and Gardens
Washington Post

McRoberts Interiors

Cheryl McRoberts
43 E. Jefferson St.
Naperville, IL 60540
(708) 420-2141

Testimonial:
"Cheryl is an extremely talented and artistically creative designer who is able to transform what a client has only imagined into an intimate personal environment with an understated elegance that truly stands the test of time."

Philosophy:
We recognize that each client is unique; therefore, we feel that it is important to reach an in-depth understanding of the client's needs, desires and lifestyle.

We are committed to producing an interior environment that reflects the essence of the client while maintaining integrity of design.

Client List:
Private Residences: Chicago, IL; Lake Geneva, WI; Florida; Providence, RI; Sacramento and Palo Alto, CA; Toronto, Calgary, CANADA.

Commercial Work: Retirement and Geriatric Center, Veterinary Animal Hospital, Optometrist Showroom and Office, Financial Services Offices, Corporate Offices, Retail Jeweler.

Professional Affiliations:
ASID

Education, Awards, Etc.:
Iowa State University, B.S., 1965
Iowa State University, M.A., 1973
Iowa State University Design Advisory Board, 1984 through present.

Publications:
Chicago Tribune
Chicago Sun Times
Veterinary Economics Magazine
The Designer

Rose Interiors, Ltd.

Marilyn Rose, ASID
7013 N. Tripp Ave.
Lincolnwood, IL 60646
(708) 677-5984

Testimonial:
"Drama and an exquisite sense of style are hallmarks of an interior designed by Marilyn Rose. Her creativity and her knack of uncovering the beautiful and unusual has enriched our environment. In short, she has given us a home to treasure for years to come."
     Client
     Chicago, IL

Philosophy:
Commitment to the client and our concern that the client receives the best we can offer in interior design is our primary interest. The challenge is in creating a beautiful environment that functions within the parameters of the client's lifestyle, taste and needs. We enjoy the variety offered us working with both residential and commercial projects. Design work that is timeless and exciting, that shows attention to detail and conveys a real sense of care is synonymous with Rose Interiors, Ltd.

Client List:
Private Residences: Chicago Gold Coast, North Shore; North and South Florida; Connecticut; Phoenix, Arizona.

Commercial Work: Corporate Offices, Private Boat, Funeral Home, Retail Store, Display.

Professional Affiliations:
American Society of Interior Designers
Professional Affiliate of the American Institute of Architects

Education, Awards, Etc.
University of Illinois, Chicago Academy of Fine Art; practicing in the Chicago area since 1967; President of the Illinois Chapter of ASID 1988, 1989; ASID Interior Design Honor Award, ASID Community Service Award, ASID Distinguished Service Award, ASID Chapter Presidential Citation

Publications:
Chicago Tribune
Chicago Sun Times
Kitchen and Bath Concepts
The Designer
Advertising Age
What Do You Say to a Naked Room
     by Catherine Crane

Robert J. Melin, Ltd.

Robert J. Melin, ASID
1352 N. LaSalle St.
Chicago, IL 60610
(312) 280-6900

Testimonial:
"When I interviewed four designers and decided to work with Bob, I knew instantly that choosing him was right. My townhouse needed full design work. Bob was able to plan a comprehensive scheme to include the art and furnishings that I already owned. Of course, we added a good amount of new things. His approach was creative and unique. His sense of color and balance is fantastic. He miraculously put together a beautiful gallery of art and furniture in a comfortable and wonderful way!
        Daniel Cotter, President
        Cotter & Company

Philosophy:
Good interior design is the result of positive relationships between the client and the designer. It is my responsibility to shape the interiors so that the environment reflects the lifestyle and personality of each client. As a practicing professional for many years, I believe that successful design means strong creative talent and sound business-sense. As an individual, I am very sensitive to the elements and beauty of an interior space. Consequently, I have always maintained offices in my residence. This enables me to be within a creative environment at all times.

Client List:
Private residences and offices in the Chicago area, New York, California, Florida, Michigan, Wisconsin and Canada.

Professional Affiliations:
ASID

Awards, Etc.:
Designer of Merit Award for Residential Design by the Design Resource Council, The Merchandise Mart, 1985.
Artwork exhibited at the Craft Museum in New York, Smithsonian Institute in Washington, D.C., and Cranbrook Academy in Bloomfield Hills, Michigan.

Publications:
His work has appeared in numerous publications.

Photo Credits:
Steve Hall, HedrichBlessing

Doris Oster Interiors

DORIS OSTER INTERIORS
211 EAST CHICAGO AVENUE
CHICAGO, ILLINOIS 60611

211 East Chicago Avenue
Suite 920
Chicago, IL 60611
(312) 664-1660
Fax: 312-664-9560

Testimonial:
"Besides the talent and fine reputation that Doris Oster Interiors has achieved over these past years, other virtues became equally as important to me. The staff had tremendous understanding and patience regarding my needs and Doris Oster's availability made me feel even more secure. This type of working atmosphere created a most enjoyable and successful result."

Philosophy:
We endeavor to seek out our client's interests, desires and needs. After establishing this information we employ our experience and skills in guiding them to achieve their goals.

The client should feel comfortable and pleased with their choice of designer. Design projects take long periods of concentrated efforts, thus an enjoyable, compatible and professional relationship should prevail at all times. A quality staff and good craftsmen are the key to the successful completion of a design project. Without this support designers cannot fulfill their commitment to the client. Design work is team work and requires multi-talented people. If the designer is confident so are the craftsmen that produce the designs.

Client List:
Private Residences: The Gold Coast, Streeterville, North Shore Suburban Chicago Area, Detroit, New York.

Commercial Work: Advertising Agencies, Condominiums, Residential Lobbies, Bank Executive Offices, Law Firms, Medical Offices, Hospitals, Olympia & York Development Company, McDonald Corporation, Summer Resorts.

Professional Affiliations:
ASID, ISID

Education, Awards, Etc.:
The Art Institute of Chicago
The Chicago Academy of Fine Arts

Publications:
Chicago Magazine
New York Times Magazine
Chicago Sun Times
Chicago Tribune
Art & Business

Inez Saunders & Associates Inc.

Inez Saunders
449 N. Wells St.
Chicago, IL 60610
(312) 329-9557

Client List:
Private Residences: Chicago, Lake Shore Drive, Gold Coast areas and other select areas of the city; North Shore suburbs; Florida, New York, Michigan, Washington, D.C.; and cities in California.

Commercial Work: Restaurants, Stores, Building Lobbies and Hallways, Model Apartments, Offices including Law, Medical, Dental, Publishers and Private Enterprises.

Education, Awards, Etc.
Inez graduated from the University of Michigan in Ann Arbor. Her associates have studied at the Art Institute of Pittsburgh, Iowa State University, Ohio State University, University of Michigan and Harrington School of Design.

Publications:
House Beautiful
House and Garden
Better Homes and Gardens
North Shore Magazine
Chicago Tribune
Chicago Sun Times

Testimonial:
"Working with Inez Saunders and the associates in her office was wonderful. Not only did they listen to our needs, but they met them with very dramatic and creative solutions. They have an excellent sense of the use of space, color, design, and specialize in lighting effects. Best of all, they met deadlines and stayed within our budget. We never could have believed furnishing our home could be such a pleasurable experience."
    A Very Satisfied Client
    Chicago, IL

Philosophy:
Every home or place of business should make a personal statement about its occupants. To discover clients' individual styles, we exchange ideas and develop new concepts to create an environment which is uniquely their own, whether contemporary, modern, traditional or any combination of furnishings.

    We also believe it is essential to maintain a high degree of professionalism in order to carry on a successful business relationship. Our office communicates well and works efficiently to keep projects flowing and to satisfy clients' needs.

    Our professional practices and dedication to the needs of our clients have earned us respect in the industry for over twenty years.

Schirn Associates, Incorporated

Janet Schirn, FASID
401 North Franklin Street
Chicago, IL 60610
(312) 222-0017

Michael Cuttie, ASID

Testimonial:
"It's incredible to me how they can visualize a finished product without seeing the original place—and have it be beautiful!"
    Mr. and Mrs. Richard Alexander

"It is all just breathtaking. We are so proud and pleased."
    Nancy and David Lawrenz

"Janet Schirn is a delight to work with. I found her taste to be impeccable. She is the ultimate professional and stayed within my budget."
    Dorothy Fuller

"Working with them was like being in a dream. I would close my eyes and envision a room—and Michael and Janet would make it come true."
    Mrs. Mark Koss

"Once you know Janet, you cannot work with anyone else. Her talent, knowledge, and professionalism as well as her sensitivity enabled us to create an environment which is preciously our own."
    Mrs. Andre Saltoun

"Janet Schirn and her staff are delightful to work with. They are truly expert in planning, color, and have just the right 'eye'."
    Mrs. Earl Deutsch

"Everyone was nutty over the lighting. You're absolutely the best."
    Mr. and Mrs. Joseph Levinson

Philosophy:
Excellence is our major commitment, both in design and service. Client objectives and attitudes are reflected in each project, creating highly individual personal expressions.

Our work is creative, sophisticated, comfortable, timeless and discriminating. Projects are architecturally oriented. Lighting is a major focus, as is the use of art.

Client List:
Private Residences: US, Great Britain, France.

Commercial Work: Ann Klein, Brunswick Corp, Biltmore Country Club, The Carlyle, Chicago White Sox, 400 East Randolph Condominium, Goodyear, Georgetown University, Holly Hunt, Metropolitan Structures, Lexington House, Masland, M & M Club, Park Astor, St. Charles, Village Smithy.

Professional Affiliations:
ASID, Fellow
AIA

Education, Awards, Etc.
Janet Schirn: Pratt Institute, BFA; Columbia University, MFA; University of Illinois, Architecture

ASID National Honor Award, Midwest Honor Awards, Illinois Designer of the Year Award; Halo Lighting Competition Honor Award; Chicago Lighting Institute Honor Awards; Who's Who; Who's Who in Interior Design; Eastman-Kodak/PPA Honor Award; Merchandise Mart Distinguished Designer Award

Michael Cuttie: Chicago Academy of Fine Arts, BFA; Loyola University; University of Lille, France; University of San Francisco, Spain

ASID: Presidential Citation, Distinguished Service Award, Education Award, Young Member Award

Publications:
House and Garden
House Beautiful
Interior Design
Interiors
The Designer
Contract
Chicago Tribune
Chicago Sun Times
New York Times

Greg Stratman Enterprises, Inc.

Greg Stratman
1032 N. LaSalle St.
Chicago, IL 60610
(312) 642-0800

Testimonial:
"An opportunity to create our own environment was not only made enjoyable, but the results far surpassed our expectations. We are still exhilarated walking through the space even after eight years."

Philosophy:
To create visually exciting solutions for each design commission through communication with the client and pulling from an architectural background that defines space rather than fill it.

Client List:
Private Residences: In and around Chicago, Palm Beach, Palm Springs, Aspen, Yachts.

Commercial Work: Restaurants for Gilbert Robinson, Don Roth, Gene Sage, Banks and Law Firms.

Professional Affiliations:
ISID

Education, Awards, Etc.
Architectural, Design and Liberal Arts background from Illinois Institute of Technology, University of Illinois and The Art Institute of Chicago.

Has been a practicing designer for 20 years—the last 12 in his own business.

1984-Rising Talent Design Award. 1984-Chicago Tribune recognition as 1 of 5 top designers in Chicago.

Publications:
Chicago Tribune
Chicago Tribune Sunday Magazine
Chicago Sun Times
Crain's Chicago Business
Parade Magazine
Town and Country
Hospitality
Interior Design
North Shore Magazine

Howard Alan Zaltzman Interior Design, Ltd.

Howard A. Zaltzman, ISID
1240 Somerset Ave.
Deerfield, IL 60015
(708) 948-5734

Testimonial:
"What seems to be most important to Howard is how comfortable we will be with the finished product. He does not do a room with the goal of making his own distinct design statement. On the contrary, the room must reflect his client's needs and wishes. To this end, Howard was a pleasure and joy to work with, and we are still most delighted with the outcome."
    Client
    Glencoe, IL

Philosophy:
I endeavor to make the entire design process as easy and enjoyable for the client as possible. The finished product is most important, but getting to the end result should be a pleasurable experience for the client, and not a nightmare of unanswered phone calls and broken promises.

Client List:
Private Residences: Private clients in Winnetka, Glencoe, Wilmette, Highland Park, Northbrook, Deerfield, and Chicago, Illinois as well as in Boca Raton, Florida and Palm Springs, California.

Commercial Work: Commercial work for Law Offices in Chicago, Dental Offices in Skokie, Pension Planner Offices in Northbrook, and Country Club in Homewood Flossmoor.

Professional Affiliations:
ISID

Education, Awards, Etc.:
BS in Economics from the Wharton School of the University of Pennsylvania/Graduated from the Harrington Institute of Interior Design with Diploma in Interior Design.

SHOWCASE
OF
INTERIOR DESIGN
RESOURCES

Showcase of Interior Design
invites you to contemplate the
special world of fine material
and craftsmanship reserved for
the professional interior designer
and his clients. These are
manufacturers who design products
for the home which are
specifically marketed to the
design trade. Their collections are
generally more rarified than the
selection of products available
through retail stores. The variety
of options such as finishes,
colors, patterns and sizes place
many in a category which might
be termed "custom".

These collections are
lavishly presented in Chicago's
great Art Deco landmark,
The Merchandise Mart. Many
showrooms offer
professionally designed galleries
which instruct and inspire
visitors. If, as the poet Goethe observed,
"Taste is only to be
educated by contemplation,"
a tour of The Mart with
an interior designer is an
education in itself.

Due to the vast array
of designs offered and the great
number of options presented
with each, the process of selecting
can be intimidating.
Showroom personnel are trained
to discuss their products
and ordering procedures in
professional terms with designers,
architects or retailers. This is the
underlying reason why, as
wholesale buying centers,
these showrooms do not sell
directly to the consumer.
However, all of the interior
designers in this edition of
Showcase of Interior Design
have the credentials and
experience to help you sort through
the alternatives. They will help
you discover designs which
will fulfill your most subtle and
personal expectations.

Baker, Knapp & Tubbs
6-187 The Merchandise Mart
Chicago, IL 60654
(312) 337-7144

Graham & Burnham Antiques

1280 Merchandise Mart
Chicago, IL 60654
(312) 822-0876

"…our gallery offers to designers and their clients a beautiful and diverse collection of fine 18th and 19th century English and French antiques—both formal and country pieces, personally selected for their individuality and suitability in today's eclectic interiors…"

Susan Graham, Owner

"…interspersed throughout our showroom are examples of Cocheo's superb artistry in custom upholstered furniture, underscoring our commitment to the highest quality…"

Bruce Burnham, Owner

Frederick Cooper

2545 W. Diversey Avenue
Chicago, IL 60647
(312) 384-0800

Importers of Classic
Oriental Rugs
The Merchandise Mart
Suite 1378
Chicago, IL 60654
(312) 670-0120

The Designer's Oriental
Rug Source.

Selection. That's always the most challenging part of picking an oriental rug. Where do you go to find a rug with that perfect green somewhere between celadon and sea foam? Where do you go to find antique rugs larger than 12' x 15'—enough to truly have a

choice? Where do you go to find superior examples of every kind of oriental rug, whether new, semi-antique or antique?

At Jorian our sole purpose is to serve as the designer's oriental rug source.

Interior Design by Interiors II Ltd., Chicago

O Merchandise Mart
hicago, IL 60654
12) 527-4141

More than three million
decision-makers shop
The Merchandise Mart in
Chicago each year—design
professionals who bring their
corporate and consumer clients
to choose from thousands of
furnishings options.

To stroll The Mart's cor-
ridors is to enjoy a treasure
trove of sophisticated design to
suit any style of contemporary
and traditional home and office
decor. Thousands of show-
rooms with tens of thousands
of lines for every room, every
use; rugs, carpeting and hard-
surface floorings; textiles; window and wallcoverings of every
kind; bath and kitchen fixtures
and furnishings; lighting; and
a wealth of decorative accessories are on display, many of
them in captivating vignettes or
room settings.

Rosemark Designs, Inc.

Meredith A. Campbell,
 Allied Member ASID
James W. Doyle,
 Allied Member ASID
210 West Campus Drive,
 Arlington Heights, Illinois 60004
(708) 253-1106

Bernard Nusinow Interior Design, © Paul Schlisman, photography

Window treatments will enhance any design project. They can serve as a soft backdrop to highlight a beautifully decorated room or they can be the focal point of elegant surroundings. Magnificent fabric in gently flowing cascades and jabots will present a warm and inviting retreat from our hectic daily lives.

Bed treatments and dressings, either in a simple Contemporary line, a lavish Victorian or Traditional style can present a very sophisticated look and comfort to any room. Properly done, in addition to the practical aspects of privacy and light control, window and bed treatments can make a dramatic statement of your own personal preference in taste and lifestyle.

Rosemark Designs accomplishes all this with old world craftsmanship and techniques, unique in today's hi-tech society. Professionalism and expertise in every area of our organization is what makes the difference in the completed design project. It is total dedication to ''Professionalism'' in serving the most discerning clients through the most prestigious designers that makes Rosemark the ''Professionals to the Profession.''

Lori Lennon & Associates, design, © Paul Schlisman, photography

Select from an extensive array of original designs in sling, strap, and cushion styles. Fabricated from extruded aluminum for maximum strength, all pieces are powder-coated for exceptional life, and com plemented with distinctive fabrics. Call for your free, full color Trop-itone Outdoor Furniture catalog, or for The Veneman Collection catalog featuring singular styles in cast-aluminum.

SHOWCASE
OF
INTERIOR DESIGN
RESOURCES

The following resources
have generously sponsored
and facilitated distribution of
Showcase of Interior Design.
Their distinguished products and
services are available through
professional interior designers
and architects.

KNAPP & TUBBS

EXECUTIVE OFFICE

FREDERICK
COOPER

GRAHAM & BURNHAM Antiques

Importers of Classic Oriental Rugs

Rosemark Designs, Inc

Probably the finest.

INDEX
RESIDENTIAL
INTERIOR
DESIGNERS

INDEX
COMMERCIAL
INTERIOR
DESIGNERS

INDEX
OF
PHOTOGRAPHERS

Please send me _____ copies of
Showcase of Interior Design
at $36.00 plus $3. each for
postage and handling.

☐ Check is enclosed.   Amount enclosed _____

Name_____

Title_____

Company_____

Address_____

City_____

State_____Zip_____

Phone_____

I would like more information about the following Interior Designers.

_____

_____

_____

_____

_____

_____

Name_____

Title_____

Company_____

Address_____

City_____

State_____Zip_____

Phone_____

I would like more information about the following Interior Designers.

_____

_____

_____

_____

_____

_____

Name_____

Title_____

Company_____

Address_____

City_____

State_____Zip_____

Phone_____

NO POSTAGE
NECESSARY
IF MAILED
IN THE
UNITED STATES

BUSINESS REPLY MAIL
FIRST CLASS MAIL   PERMIT NO 6475   GRAND RAPIDS MI

POSTAGE WILL BE PAID BY ADDRESSEE

**VITAE PUBLISHING COMPANY INC
800 GRAND PLAZA PLACE
220 LYON ST NW
GRAND RAPIDS MI 49502-3189**

NO POSTAGE
NECESSARY
IF MAILED
IN THE
UNITED STATES

BUSINESS REPLY MAIL
FIRST CLASS MAIL   PERMIT NO 6475   GRAND RAPIDS MI

POSTAGE WILL BE PAID BY ADDRESSEE

**VITAE PUBLISHING COMPANY INC
800 GRAND PLAZA PLACE
220 LYON ST NW
GRAND RAPIDS MI 49502-3189**

NO POSTAGE
NECESSARY
IF MAILED
IN THE
UNITED STATES

BUSINESS REPLY MAIL
FIRST CLASS MAIL   PERMIT NO 6475   GRAND RAPIDS MI

POSTAGE WILL BE PAID BY ADDRESSEE

**VITAE PUBLISHING COMPANY INC
800 GRAND PLAZA PLACE
220 LYON ST NW
GRAND RAPIDS MI 49502-3189**